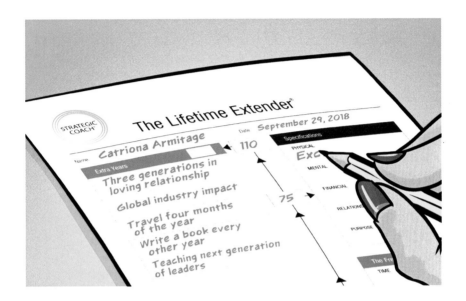

Download your PDF copy of our Lifetime Extender thinking process at *strategiccoach.com/go/156* before reading this stimulating little book.

A uniquely integrated way of using a new life extension goal to increasingly transform all of your thinking about your past, present, and future.

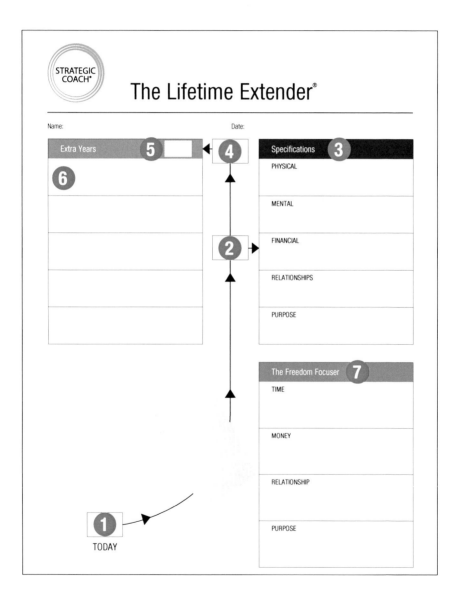

1. Your age today

Start The Lifetime Extender exercise by writing your present age in the box located in the lower left corner.

2. The age at which you expect to die

Next, write down the age at which you expect to die. This might be based on averages, family history, etc.

3. Your "how you want to be" specifications

Write down five specifications regarding how you want want to be—physically, mentally, financially, relationship-wise, and in terms of your purpose—*the year before* you expect to die.

4. Your extended age

Answer this question: If these five things were true the year before you expected to die, what are the chances you would actually die in the next year? Do you think you might live longer? How many years longer than you expected? Add this amount to the age at which you expected to die. Write your new number in the top box.

5. Your "extra years"

Write down the number of additional years you chose in the "Extra Years" box.

6. "Extra years" goals

Now that you've created these additional years in your mind, reinforce the vision of your extended lifetime by listing five achievements that will now be possible because you've given yourself significantly more time. What do you want to do in your extra years?

7. Your expanding freedom

To wrap up this exercise, define how your extended lifetime and "extra years" achievements will expand your personal freedom in the four crucial areas of Time, Money, Relationship, and Purpose.

This exercise will immediately and automatically change how you make use of your present capabilities, resources, and opportunities to achieve the bigger and better future that will be the result of living an extended lifetime. Doing this exercise will multiply the impact of reading this book.

MY PLAN FOR LIVING TO 156

Text **60 Minutes**	The length of our small books is based on the time in the air of a flight between Toronto and Chicago. Start reading as you take off and finish the book by the time you land. Just the right length for the 21st-century reader.
Cartoons **30 Minutes**	You can also gain a complete overview of the ideas in this book by looking at the cartoons and reading the captions. We find the cartoons have made our Strategic Coach concepts accessible to readers as young as eight years old.
Audio **120 Minutes**	The audio recording that accompanies this book is not just a recitation of the printed words but an in-depth commentary that expands each chapter's mindset into new dimensions. Download the audio at **strategiccoach.com/go/156**.
Video **30 Minutes**	Our video interviews about the concepts in the book deepen your understanding of the mindsets. If you combine text, cartoons, audio, and video, your understanding of the ideas will be 10x greater than you would gain from reading only. Watch the videos at **strategiccoach.com/go/156**.
Scorecard **10 Minutes**	Fold out the back cover of this book to score your Lifetime Extender mindset. First, score yourself on where you are now, and then fill in where you want to be a year from now. Download additional copies at **strategiccoach.com/go/156**.
ebook **1 Minute**	After absorbing the fundamental ideas of The Lifetime Extender concept, you can quickly and easily share them by sending the ebook version to as many other individuals as you desire. Direct them to **strategiccoach.com/go/156**.

Thanks to the Creative Team:

Adam Morrison

Kerri Morrison

Hamish MacDonald

Shannon Waller

Jennifer Bhatthal

Victor Lam

Margaux Yiu

Christine Nishino

Willard Bond

Peggy Lam

My Plan For Living To 156

Most people's notion about how long they're going to live is an oppressive thought. They feel confined by a certain number of years, an age expectation based on family history and averages. But what if you could extend your lifetime? How would adding extra years impact the way you live now?

My goal of living to 156 may sound outrageous at the outset. But in reading this book, I think you'll find that the imagination can have a huge impact on our behavior, and a simple mindset shift can literally change every thought in your brain.

Cartoons by Hamish MacDonald.

Printed in Toronto, Canada. The Strategic Coach Inc., 33 Fraser Avenue, Suite 201, Toronto, Ontario, M6K 3J9.

If you would like further information about The Strategic Coach® Program or other Strategic Coach® services and products, please telephone 416.531.7399 or 1.800.387.3206.

Library of Congress Control Number: 2019943824
Author Academy Elite, Powell, Ohio

Contents

Introduction
How I Chose 156
You recognize that, consciously or unconsciously, there's an age at which you expect to die and it impacts how you live your life now.

There were several things that led me to decide to expand my lifespan.

In the 1980s, there were a lot of articles coming out that questioned the fairly fixed number of years that the average person was expected to live, and these got me thinking about my own expectations regarding longevity.

There had been significant advancements in hygiene, and there were readily available pharmaceuticals that were allowing us to live longer. I also considered the factor that people in my family tend to live until their late eighties or early nineties.

I like to question fixed beliefs—not because I'm a rebel against them, but just because I try to figure out how ideas become beliefs.

How far can I go?
From a very young age, I've had an internal mindset about going as far as I can go.

As the year 2000 approached, people were talking about how those born in 1901 were going to see the end of the 20th century, and I thought, "It would be really neat to live through a calendar century." I was too late to do that with the 20th century because I was born in 1944, so I decided that I'd like to live through the entire 21st century. And so my new lifetime goal became 156.

Lots of time left.

I consciously wondered what would happen to my thinking if instead of seventy-five or eighty, I talked myself into thinking of my lifespan as 156 years. In doing so, I found that every time I thought about my lifespan, it made me feel young.

I started to feel I had an enormous amount of time available to me, but I'd noticed the opposite happening to people in the business community who were in their forties and fifties: they felt that they were getting old and running out of time.

I don't like the thought of feeling older and that there are things I won't be able to do because I don't have enough time left to do them. I decided to leverage this thought of 156 into always feeling that I'm young and that I have an enormous amount of time left. I could start whole new projects and have big goals.

This number has changed all the other thoughts I've had in my life.

You have a number.

In the fall of 1993, I tried out the idea on one of my workshop groups, calling it The Lifetime Extender.

It was very simple. I just said, "I want you to write down the age at which you're going to die." Everybody wrote down a number. And then I asked, "Why did you write down that number?" For a lot of people, their number was based on family history as well as the averages of when people tend to die.

The numbers ranged from early fifties to 100 years old, but everybody, whether they'd thought about it before or not, had an answer to the question of when they were going to die.

The next question I asked was, "Is that a number you agree with, or would you like to have another number?" I've never met a person who doesn't choose to extend their number once they've identified it. And I've seen that this choice to give themselves more years immediately impacts how they're living in the present.

Extend your lifespan.
It was discovered at some point that the average life insurance agent actually died about ten years earlier than the average buyer of life insurance.

This is because the agents believe in the actuarial tables— which to me are just an average of when people have died— more than the customers did.

Similarly, doctors die earlier than patients do because they're more in touch with all of the things that can kill you; whereas, the average person doesn't think about these things until they actually become a problem.

There are mindsets that encourage you to live as long as you possibly can, and there are mindsets that almost have you talk yourself into dying earlier than is necessary.

Change your present.
The biggest impact of committing yourself to a longer lifespan is that it changes how you live your present day.

A lot of people have asked me if I really think that I'm going to live to 156. My answer is that I know I won't if I don't have it as a goal, and the big issue actually isn't whether I make it to that age. If I'm interrupted, who cares? There are those who think I'm setting myself up for disappointment, but I'm pretty confident that once I'm gone, it won't bother me!

But it's profoundly affected how I live my life in the present. I've noticed a big difference in how I live my life in my seventies compared to how other people in their seventies live, when they're expecting to die within the next decade.

Focusing on health.
Once you decide to extend your lifespan, you start taking health more seriously. There's a market for products and services for people who'd like to live longer than was the norm in the past, and the biggest technological breakthrough has been the internet, where you can just plug in questions about breakthroughs in the field of health.

There are now clinics and networks of specialists whose focus is what's called regenerative health, which is looking into whether the aging process can be corrected physiologically.

I'm all eyes and ears when it comes to these kinds of things because I have that 156-year goal.

Strangely enough, by having a number that's further off in the future, you take the present day experience you have available to you now more seriously. You get more focused on the real meaning and value of your present circumstances.

Chapter 1
The Lifetime Extender

You understand that the age at which you expect to die is negotiable — and changing your future number changes your present.

What I'm going to do now is take you through the process, as I've done at the beginning of very many workshops, for extending what you expect to be your lifespan. You can download copies of the exercise at *strategiccoach.com/go/156.*

Taking this time to focus on your future will have immediate enormous and positive effects on how you live your life in the present.

To start off, write down the number that represents the age at which you expect to die. Answer spontaneously. Consciously or unconsciously, you have a number in mind. Everybody does. This number will be based on family history, your own health, your observations of those around you, and your beliefs about longevity.

In your final year.
I'm not going to talk about the age you just wrote down; I'm going to talk about the year before that age.

I want you to answer five questions about what you want your life to be like the year before you die:

1. How are you doing physically?
2. How are you doing mentally?
3. How are you doing financially?
4. How would you describe the quality of your relationships?
5. What's your assessment of the life you've led up until this time?

I've been asking entrepreneurs these questions for over 25 years, and the answers have been consistent:

"I'm in great shape with lots of energy, I'm mentally sharp and excited about intellectual challenges, I'm financially independent, I'm totally engaged in my many warm and supportive relationships, and I'm very satisfied with the life I've led up to this point."

Living longer.

The answers to those questions might be significantly different if I posed them about your present, but I'm presenting you with your future possibilities, so it makes sense that you imagine being on top of and satisfied in all of these categories.

My next question is, "If your life were as you described, what do you think the chances are that you would die the very next year?"

Likely, you wouldn't.

So then, barring the occurrence of random accidents and unforeseen circumstances, how many years longer than your initial answer do you think you would live?

Adding to the number.

Most often, people's answer to that last question is, "I'd live for another ten or 15 years."

But I'm going to ask you to be specific. If that's your answer, then which is it? Ten more years or 15 more years? Or another amount entirely? Write this down. Now, you have a new number. We've gone from one specific age at which you expect to die to a different, higher one.

Subtract your first answer from your new number, and consider the resulting number. We're just partway through this short exercise, and you've already bought that many more years of life.

From this point forward, when you think of when you're going to die, you won't be able to think of that first number you wrote down; you'll always think of the new number. And this change is going to impact every other thought you have.

In your extra years.
Now that you have those extra years, ask yourself what you really want to do with them. Write down the specific activities you'd like to be doing if you were free to do whatever you wanted.

Take the time to think about it, and make a list of all those activities you never thought you'd get the chance to do.

Something interesting I've noticed is that very few people put down work-related activities here. It's most often that entrepreneurs want to use their extra years for activities like learning a new language, doing charitable work, taking up hobbies, and doing a lot of traveling.

Whatever it is that you want to spend those years doing, these are goals that probably just a minute ago, you didn't think you would have the time in your life to do. But now, because of your new way of thinking, you have more than enough time. There's a spaciousness to your life now because of this mindset shift.

Bonus time starts now.

So far, you've created some extra years for yourself, and you've determined what it is that you want to get done during those extra years.

The question to answer now—and it's a big one—is this: "When do you want to take these extra years?"

Most people answer that they want to take the extra years, in which they'll do all of those activities that they listed, right now.

If you want to take the extra years you've created for yourself now, then, starting immediately, you're in what you can think of as bonus time, because up until now, you didn't have all of these years available to you.

You now have the years, and you have the goals that you said you want to achieve in this time. So, how are you going to arrange your life now? With this mindset shift, you can start to realize that you're not just putting in time till you retire at sixty-five and then do all the things you actually really care about. You can start doing those things right now.

Finally, consider how this extended lifetime might affect your sense of freedom in terms of your time, money, relationships, and purpose. As your sense of your lifetime expands, your freedom will too.

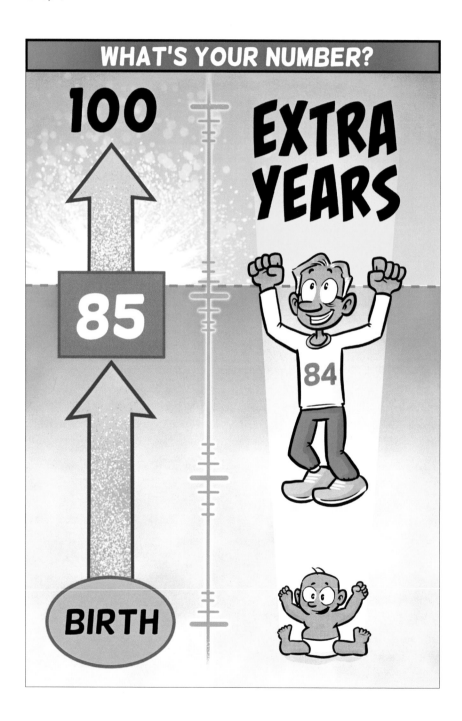

THE YEAR BEFORE

PHYSICALLY	"IN GREAT SHAPE, LOTS OF ENERGY"
MENTALLY	"SHARP, FOCUSED, FEELING POSITIVE"
FINANCIALLY	"INDEPENDENT, NO WORRIES AT ALL"
RELATIONSHIPS	"MANY, DEEP, WARM, SUPPORTIVE"
ASSESSMENT	"TOTALLY PROUD AND SATISFIED"

Chapter 2
Everybody Has A Number
You confidently choose the extended age at which you'll die and then use that number to transform everything else.

There was an early client of Strategic Coach who literally jumped when I asked him to write down the age at which he expected to die. I remarked that he seemed to have a strong response to this and asked him what his number was. It was 47. I asked him, "How old are you?" and he said, "Forty-six."

I asked why 47 was his number, and he replied, "There isn't a male member of my family in the last two generations who lived past forty-seven."

I asked this client how he was doing now compared to how he'd want to be living in the year before he died. He told me that everything he was doing was setting himself up to die at forty-seven. He said, "I'm 50 pounds overweight, I don't exercise, and I drink heavily." He hadn't made any new friends in the last five years, and he wasn't taking on any new interests.

He hadn't been conscious of it before I asked him the question, but he'd been living based on his number; part of his brain just didn't see anything beyond forty-seven. When I asked him the question to make him conscious of it, it shocked him.

Being clear it's yours.
I later saw him when he was sixty. He told me then that he'd never had very good relationships, but that he'd been in a really solid relationship for the past ten years—which means

that it started three years after the age he'd stopped planning beyond.

The Lifetime Extender exercise both extended his life and improved how he was living once he changed his number to the one that was right for him.

The lifetime goal that you choose has to feel right to you, whether it makes sense to anyone else or not. How every person thinks about the life they've lived, and their expectations for their lives in the future, is unique, and it's not something that anyone else can experience.

Each of us lives in a vast, secret universe in which we make goals that others don't know about. The important thing is to end up on the number that feels good and right to you.

Everybody has a number, and when they go through the exercise, it becomes clear that the number they originally had in mind wasn't really their number because they ended up changing it. It's only maybe one out of every hundred people that doesn't change their number when given the opportunity.

Most people just go along.
The vast majority of other people have given themselves an age limitation based on what other people believed and accepted was possible. There's the way you think about things, and then there's how other people think you should be thinking about things.

For a lot of people, the latter has more weight than their own thinking.

Even just from a genetic standpoint, we're not all created equal, so the "rules" about lifespan automatically don't apply to everyone. And as we've discussed, the attitude of an individual can have an effect on their lifespan, as well as on how they live in their present day.

Number that changes everything.
Consciously changing what you think of as the number of years in your lifetime reveals how you think about everything connected to your past, present, and future and causes your thinking to change.

You don't have to work at this. The change in number is what brings on the changes in thinking, because you immediately discover that the thoughts and plans you had were based on your previous thinking about how long you were going to live.

It might be that you would have done some things differently if you'd had your new number in mind earlier, but more importantly, you'll discover that some thoughts you've had about your present and future only made sense with your initial number, and things are different for you now.

It's likely that whether you knew it or not, you were having thoughts and plans that centered on preparing to die at that earlier age.

Stop getting ready to die.
Whatever thoughts you've had about the inevitability of death can now fade away and be replaced by thoughts about the extension of life. This trade has a profound impact.

An example for me is that I now spend the first two hours of every day burning calories and exercising muscles, because this daily action is necessary for my lifetime extension.

It's really a matter of self-efficacy; if you think you're going to die, you will, and if you think you're going to live, you will.

Death has been around for a long time, and it's very good at what it does. It doesn't need any help from me, and it's not going to get it.

Your brain naturally goes to what your most important focus is, who you spend time with, what you're interested in, what you're not interested in, and what your activities are, and this is all organized by an expectation.

If you're expecting something, you're going to gather as much information as possible about it. So, if you're expecting death, you'll have thoughts about death, and if you're expecting lifetime extension, your thoughts will circle around lifetime extension.

Suddenly, you get extra years.
Your decision to extend your lifetime immediately gives you a sense of having "extra years" right now. The extra years aren't coming to you when you're a teenager; you're getting these extra years now that you've had an enormous amount of life experience.

Just as you already had a number in mind for your death, whether you were conscious of it or not, you already know what you'd most like to get done during these years, which until very recently weren't available to you. A whole new world of possibilities can now open up for you.

Chapter 3
Ignoring Others' Expectations

You pay no attention to how long other people expect to live or what they think about your goal for a longer life.

The worst decade of my life was between the ages of thirty and forty, and it had to do with the fact that I just wasn't saying what I wanted. I've since translated a lot of loss into learning in my mind, but the experience was grueling. I hit a lot of obstacles, but eventually I came to grips with who I was and what I really wanted in life.

The area of expected lifespan is highly individual. Once you have your chosen number, you have a permanently independent point of reference in your thinking. It's completely yours, and yours alone, and so all of your thinking becomes independent of other people's thinking about how you should be living and how you should be thinking.

Entirely new way of thinking.

Your new Lifetime Extender number will increasingly enable you to think about everything else in your life from a fresh perspective.

When I have a new thought, I bounce it off of 156, and this immediately puts me in a realm that no one else is thinking about. Having that long-term goal as a concept to bounce today's decisions off of has quite a profound impact.

One of my biggest objectives is to be increasingly useful to the people around me, and that means I have to get better in the areas where I'm really good, and get out of the way in areas where others are really good so that I can support their growth. But I doubt I'd be thinking this way if my number indicated that I should be wrapping things up in my career now.

Avoiding the "retirement" trap.

One of the most important things you can do for yourself is avoid the whole notion of retirement. The entire idea of retirement means that you'd be no longer growing, no longer useful, and simply getting ready to die. Why would you think this way at all?

What a lot of people don't know is that the political reason for the creation of retirement in the 19th century was the fear of Marxism.

German Chancellor Otto von Bismarck realized that those most likely to become Marxist revolutionaries were young, unemployed men, so they created a system called retirement in order to get the older people out of the marketplace to make room for the younger men. It's an old concept that isn't relevant in the same way today—and isn't relevant at all for entrepreneurs.

When people talk about retirement, they start talking themselves into an early grave. They stop learning new things, stop developing new things, stop building relationships, and stop meeting new people.

Retiring at a certain age has become normal in society, but with your Lifetime Extender thinking, you can now see that there's no reason why you should have that mindset.

Don't talk yourself into being taken out of use, and don't talk yourself into dying early.

Becoming younger as you age.

When I coach a workshop now, I might be decades older than many people in the room, but when I'm speaking to someone who's 50 years younger than I am, I'm intensely interested in how they're looking at the world.

There's a big difference in our ages, but they're human beings who have the same drive to improve themselves as I do.

When you do The Lifetime Extender exercise, you start noticing that people who haven't gone through this change in thinking talk as though they believe that their past is bigger than their future. If your thoughts aren't about a bigger, more exciting, unpredictable future, then you're stuck in the past with no way to grow. This is no way to live what could be the most innovative, creative years of your life.

Science supports your plan.

Because of your Lifetime Extender thinking, you'll be increasingly aware of the scientific and technological breakthroughs taking place in the area of human longevity.

The work that people are doing, the discoveries they're making, and the new capabilities they're creating all support my plan to live to 156. There's this massive amount of new support, and it gets better each year.

If you were the only one thinking along these lines, it would be tougher, but you'll benefit from other people's interest in the topic. The world at its most alert, curious, responsive, and resourceful is 100 percent on the side of your plan to live longer.

Unique here, unique everywhere.
With The Lifetime Extender, you now have an entirely new and unique way of thinking about your past, present, and future because you're no longer thinking about your lifespan in a conventional way. Because you have uniquely extended your future expectations, you're also uniquely thinking about everything else in that future.

It was six years before I told anyone about my Lifetime Extender idea in order to see if it was a thought I could stick with, and what happened was that the thought got stronger and stronger.

Within one year, the 156 thought had replaced all other thoughts, and I started noticing the difference in how I was thinking about everything else.

When you change that number, you change every other thought you have, and the way you're changing is independent of the way other people are treating those thoughts. So it makes you more and more creative as you go along because you're less and less influenced by other people's notions and expectations.

What's generally true doesn't have to be specifically true. Do most people die around age eighty? Yes, but that has no bearing on what's going to be specifically true about you.

For most people, they have a number but it's not useful to them. What you're doing is turning your number into one of the most useful thoughts you have. And it's all completely unique to you.

You're not just living longer, you're living differently.

Chapter 4
Friends, Money, And Purpose
You continually expand three crucial daily capabilities for living a longer life.

When people think about longevity, they tend to think about health issues—a topic that's endless because there are always new breakthroughs in this area.

But three things predispose people to being able to see themselves continuing on into the future: friends, money, and purpose. You need these to have the desire to physically keep going, and it's our thinking that tells or doesn't tell our bodies to start dying.

The most important of these is the first, friends, because we are who we are because of who we're friends with. It's important to always be replenishing your set of friends, and to make sure not to stick just to your age group. When your friends are all your own age and they start dying, it's depressing and makes you feel that checking out soon is inevitable for you too.

When you don't have the second thing, money, it means that people have to support you, and you feel dependent. No one wants to feel like a burden to others. And the third category, purpose, means having something to live for. It's necessary to have something to keep you going, that gives your life meaning.

Appreciation, support, and fun.
We're human only to the degree that we're social. We think of ourselves as individuals, but the usefulness of our uniqueness is its impact on other people.

The only way to know that something's useful is if it's useful to others. The proof is in their appreciation of it.

I'm useful at certain things, but for a lot of other things, I require the capabilities and insights of others. I'm massively supported by other people's intelligence and creativity. Being alone with my capabilities doesn't have meaning to me.

Also, I'm noticing that the people I'm interacting with are improving, and being around people who are growing gives me enormous joy and inspiration. It pushes me to keep up with them, because I don't want to be left behind. It's the perfect environment for me to be constantly urged on by the growth of others, and I contribute to their growth, so it's reciprocal.

Being an admired hero.

We all want to be admired by an increasing number of unique individuals whose own capabilities, progress, and achievements inspire and motivate us.

No one can be a lonely hero, because you can only be a hero in a crowd.

Nothing keeps you more excited about living longer than the strategy of having greater applause in the future, and you'll also be applauding the people who are applauding you. I might be a hero to a lot of people, but those people also have to be heroes to me.

When you're a hero, you're doing something different and

better than others have seen before, but once they see it, they're inspired to go in that direction too. And when they do, they do it in a different way than you did, so you're learning new things from their growth, which you inspired.

Moving forward by writing checks.
To have constantly growing capabilities, money is required.

Essentially, every aspect of owning a growing business, including having employees with growing capabilities, requires you to write a check. The same is true for other areas of your life.

For my plan to live to 156, I need a supply of money that will allow me to take advantage of every health opportunity that comes along.

Money is a capability. The moment you start treating it as a possession, you start dying.

Making important things better.
Make sure you're clear about what's really important to you now, because that's what gives you a sense of purpose, and you want those things to be more important to you in the future.

Your sense of everything that's important to you will keep clarifying your best thinking, focusing your best abilities, and maximizing your best teamwork to make it continually more useful and enjoyable.

It's hard to have a growing sense of importance in the future unless that includes other people who are very close and connected to you. I can't imagine having a purpose that's isolated from my relationships.

I'm working hard on my health and fitness because there's a growing number of people who want me to stay energetic and alive.

More and more, I see my future as my growing capabilities interacting with other people's growing capabilities. And as long as that's expanding, there's no thought in my mind that I'm getting close to the end.

Why leave early from a party that just keeps getting better?

Future always bigger than the past.
Each day can be used to transform more of your past experiences into an exponentially more productive future for yourself and many others. I immediately take past events and transform them into raw material. I don't have a nostalgic bone in my body.

The past is simply your interpretation of results. No two people see a past event in the same way. We all make up our pasts just like we make up our futures.

You can get infinitely more use out of your past if you don't think of things as being static but rather in terms of how they can be useful going ahead.

I have no emotional connection with the past, only with what's happening now and with what's being prepared for the future. This keeps me constantly looking toward a future that's always getting bigger and better.

Chapter 5
Eliminating The Idea Of Retirement
You see yourself becoming increasingly more capable, useful, and productive as your longer life expands.

Retirement is a relatively new idea in human affairs, and it's important to remember why it was invented. As mentioned in Chapter 3, it wasn't just because the government wanted to be nice to old people, but rather to avoid a social revolution.

In 1883, Otto von Bismarck determined that Germany needed to industrialize and that the way of the future was building factories and employing workers. He also noticed that young, unemployed men were the most likely to become social revolutionaries, so he put in place a system of retirement to force older workers to leave so that positions were opened up for young people to work, keeping them too occupied to revolt.

As well, older people were not always up to the challenge of physical labor that the factories demanded; the older workers knew how to do the work, but it wore them down, and someone in their fifties wasn't considered as useful as someone in their teens or twenties.

Don't be "taken out of use."
We retire factory equipment, we retire battleships, and we retire resources. The term "retirement" means to be taken out of use. By its very nature, retirement means that a decision has been made that you're no longer useful.

When sixty-five was established as the retirement age in the United States, the average lifespan in the country was fifty-eight. The government saw this as a way of taking in money that they'd never have to pay out. Retirement was created for political reasons and for reasons related to repetitive work that tires people out.

There was a 100-year period where retirement was seen as a solution for many things, but in the 21st century, it's losing its effect. And in the world of entrepreneurism, it has absolutely no meaning whatsoever. There is no mandatory retirement for entrepreneurs. There is no legal framework that requires you to stop working at a particular age. You and your clients are the only ones who can say you're useless.

You can ignore the conventional notion that everybody slows down, wears out, and stops being useful. Retirement doesn't need to apply to you; it's strictly for people who can't continually recreate themselves.

Accelerate when others stop.
When you realize that the notion of retirement is political, is tied to industrialization, and is not just something natural, your mindset about how long you'll continue to work shifts. You'll start to notice that you feel and act younger and more energized than most people your age. Getting weaker and older is for quitters, and you're a starter.

Retirement will never be forced on you, so if your plans include no longer being useful, that's a choice you're making. Your age shouldn't dictate how useful you are, and your usefulness should go beyond "keeping up."

I don't want to keep up; I want to accelerate.

Avoid slippery slopes.
Most people talk themselves into slowing down and wrap-

ping things up, but you don't have to be one of those people. Eliminate any kind of thinking and talking that would persuade you that at a certain point in your life, you're supposed to "go downhill."

There are words and phrases in popular use that make it seem acceptable for people to be less useful and capable in the future than they were in the past. I'm sure you've heard them before: things like, "I can't do that. That's a young man's game."

There's a lot of encouragement and understanding of this type of thinking, and it causes you to feel like you're on the clock—which is going to run out eventually.

Thinking this way is subscribing to the general narrative, but the general narrative doesn't apply to your specific situation as an entrepreneur. Retirement thinking is contagious, and it's reinforced in the media, but you can resist it.

Keeping everything open-ended.
Never retiring means constantly recreating yourself. And if you want to constantly recreate yourself, you have to constantly create new projects. There's no reason to concentrate on bringing all your work to completion, except to take it to a higher level.

The timing of the end of your career is not for you to say. You'll reach a point where the game runs out and then you're gone. But it's not for you to bring that on. It's not for you to say when life is up.

Always be starting new projects, investments, and relationships. Don't entertain ideas like having a "bucket list" or leaving a legacy, because those are thoughts that include your no longer having a future.

I don't closely track the impact that Strategic Coach has on the world because I'm too focused on starting new things in the best possible way and on starting things even better in the future.

Giving death no assistance.

Being fully human means continually expanding what life means. It's not getting ready for death.

The mindsets that I'm talking about in this book weren't possible a century ago. Back then, we didn't have the abilities we do now in terms of economics, in terms of choice of interesting work, and in terms of having relationships with people all over the planet. We didn't have the entrepreneurial capabilities we do now.

Now, you can commit all of your attention and energy to everything that increases your mental, emotional, and physical health and fitness. You can continually expand your life.

At some point, the whistle will blow and you'll be finished, but it's not on you to adjust your life to something that's going to happen in a split second. Death is a reality, but there's no use in spending time thinking about it. Thinking that you're running out of time is not a good way to spend your energy.

Keep expanding the possibilities of the life you have today, and tomorrow you'll have more possibilities.

Chapter 6
Ever-Expanding Happiness
You continually identify new areas of happiness in all areas of your life and work, and keep expanding them.

Unhappiness is an extremely potent thing. It has life-limiting powers. Correspondingly, happiness is just as potent, with powers to extend your life.

There is more and more research coming out in support of the theory that being happy or unhappy can be explained by what's happening chemically inside of your body.

I believe that our bodies take their cues from our minds, and, more specifically, our minds find new things outside of us that are interesting and stimulating to us and appreciate them. If your mind has an enormous amount of appreciation and value for things that are happening to you, and these feelings are growing, your body will get the instructions that things are good and that it should keep going.

There's an intricate relationship between what your mind recognizes as being worth living for and the ability of your body to let you keep on living.

Happiness can't be pursued.
If you experience life as being unhappy, and you can only predict an unhappy future, it doesn't really give you much motivation to keep going.

But if you have a sense of having a happy existence, and that your happiness is going to expand in the future, it has an enormous impact on your physical well being. It's vital to get a handle on your happiness and to know that happiness is a skill, not a result.

The pursuit of happiness is an endless effort that sees you never achieving what you want and never arriving where you want to be. Instead of going after happiness, aim for always achieving what you want to achieve, and always being where it is that you want to be.

Being where you want to be and knowing that the feeling will expand is radically different from thinking, "I'm not where I want to be, but I'm pursuing where I want to be."

Being in the latter mindset is a tremendous strain on you, and when you're thinking that way, no measurable goal will end up actually getting you to your desired destination.

Start with gratitude and expand it.

Instead of always being in a state of pursuing happiness, appreciate and expand the happiness you have. The way to develop your happiness within yourself is by being grateful. Where there's no gratitude, there's no happiness.

A synonym for gratitude is appreciation, and appreciation also has an economic definition, which is "increasing the value of." I believe that we're happy to the degree that we can increase the value of our own experience.

Gratitude is a voluntary activity. Quite simply, you can have it if you want it. You can be grateful about anything. Once you master the capability of gratitude, of always increasing the value of everything and everyone you encounter, you can expand your happiness.

You're already there—share it.

Being happy and not sharing the feeling is like having the only telephone in the world: it's useless.

Any happiness you have inside of you takes on value only to the degree that it goes outside of you, to other people. Being unhappy influences other people in a certain way, and being happy influences other people in a certain way. We're social creatures.

The big thing is the skill just to say, "I'm happy" and acknowledge that this is within your power. It's a choice. Then your mind starts providing proof of why you're happy.

If you're unhappy, you're always looking for something outside of yourself. If you're happy, it's because you found something inside of yourself. It's your ability to appreciate and be grateful for your own life.

As you're appreciating your own life, more and more there's a natural tendency to start to appreciate other people's lives. You start to appreciate your interaction and your gratitude for your interaction with other people. It's endless.

Rejuvenate everything you touch.

The activity of appreciation is energizing, not only for you but also for what you're appreciating. With your appreciation, you bring new daily energy and confidence to every activity and relationship. And the more you expand your appreciation for certain things, there's an increased meaning.

Every year, my sense of appreciation of the life I'm experiencing and creating grows, and this affects my notion of how many more years I want to keep doing this.

With a growing appreciation for the present, why would you ever want to stop? You'll want to extend the number of days you'll live, and you'll have that much more future to look forward to.

As healthy as you are happy.
Often when someone hits seventy, they start feeling like they're approaching the end of things. They stop appreciating the present, and they don't feel like they have a future to appreciate either.

Barring illness and accidents, there's no reason for this to be the case. You don't have to slow down. There's no age at which a person needs to stop appreciating their present life or to stop looking forward to having a future that's bigger than their past.

The key to health is happiness, and you have control over your happiness by increasing your gratitude and appreciation.

If you want to be happy and keep on living, never stop living in the present, and never stop expanding your appreciation of what you have available to you today. This will extend to all the connections and relationships you have with other people.

As your expanding happiness includes more and more people, you'll experience greater strength and vitality.

Chapter 7
Future Bigger Than Past

You always see and make your life ahead transformatively bigger and better than all of your previous experience.

Nobody lives in the past and nobody lives in the future.

We live only in the present, but we have ideas about what's happened before today and about what's going to happen after today. We're very selective about what our past is and what our future is.

Knowing that the past and the future are created, it's hard to really be a victim of either one. When you begin to realize that the past and the future are just ideas, you can choose to only have ideas that serve you.

The only things from my past that are useful are those that prepare me for a better present and a better future. Attitude is key here. Arrogance interferes with inner wisdom because inner wisdom depends on your not trying to prove something, but rather on trying to find out something.

Also, recognize that you're one human among many, and you have to know what wisdom is inside of you before you can know what wisdom is outside of you.

Revving up, not wearing down.

More and more, you're setting up what your experience is. As your motivation and your fascination with things in your life keep getting bigger and bigger, you can leave behind all of the conventional thoughts that people have about slowing down and declining as you get older.

I'm in my seventies now, but according to my plan to live to 156, that's just middle aged. I'm focused on health for my present and for my future, and to give one example, I'm better at doing push-ups now than I was 25 years ago.

More useful to more people.
A key way to avoid slowing down is to be useful. I'm a lot more useful to a lot more people at seventy-three than I was at fifty.

Usefulness is a way to counteract aging, and you can measure progress in every area of your life by how useful you are to other people. Being useful is easy to do; just pay attention to what it is that other people are trying to accomplish.

You have to shift away from what you want for yourself and be more and more in touch with what other people want. See what abilities and capabilities you have that line up with other people's goals and desires.

Being useful to other people always makes me feel young, and I always know that no matter how useful I am to others, I'll be even more useful to them in the future.

Expanding everyone's confidence.
The most useful thing you can do for other people is appreciate their value. When you grow and gain momentum, it has the impact of making everyone else more confident about their own bigger future.

I've always had a good grasp on generating my own personal confidence, so when I walk into a situation, my personal confidence is not a concern. What this allows me to do is to look outward and consider how I can give confidence to the activity that everybody's involved in, and give confidence to someone else who's doing the activity.

One of the things that gives people confidence is discovering something about their own experiences that they either didn't know or didn't see in a useful way. Asking open-ended questions (ones you don't know the answers to) is a great way to generate these kinds of discoveries.

If you work on doing this for long enough, it will become hardwired in you.

Everything connects and grows.
When you put yourself in a position where you're being useful to people, those around you will gain confidence. It's up to them what they do with that confidence. You're providing them with electricity, and they'll decide what use they'll put it toward.

And if it's a good relationship, they'll reciprocate in some way.

There's no end and there's no downside to friendships like this, and, more and more, your growing capabilities are going to take the form of these greater connections.

When you connect with someone, you're not just connecting with them but also with their connections. It's endless, so no matter how far your connections go today, and how many of the people you're being useful to are also being useful to you, it can be better tomorrow.

Inspired and inspiring.

In *Nicomachean Ethics*, Aristotle describes three kinds of friendship. "The friendship of utility" is one that's useful for pragmatic purposes, and "the friendship of pleasure" describes a friendship that lasts for as long as it's a pleasure to be friends. These are both considered "accidental friendships" and short-term because they're based on specific needs.

What Aristotle calls "the friendship of the good" is a long-term friendship where both people inspire improvement in the other and admire each other's goodness.

The friendship of the good is far more possible to achieve today than it used to be because we have a greater choice of whom to connect with since we're no longer limited geographically to only those who are near us. We also have greater mobility and more time and resources to put into these friendships.

Friendships with positive reciprocal benefits are an invaluable resource that can last forever no matter what turns you might take in your life or career. The reciprocal inspiration becomes the center of your life and truly valuable.

Usefulness, appreciation, creativity, and cooperation make things permanent in a world that's changing very quickly. And when you have these positive, inspiring relationships in your life, you see a bigger future opening up in front of you no matter your age.

Chapter 8
Age-Reversing Technology
Your growing motivation for living a longer, more productive life keeps enabling you to feel and act increasingly younger.

Much of the question of how long you're going to live relates heavily to scientific, technological, and medical developments. Breakthroughs in these fields are going to make it more and more possible to live longer, but the thing is, your eyes only see and your ears only hear what your brain is looking for.

It's only because you have the goal of living longer that you're going to pick up on the phenomenal scientific, technological, and medical breakthroughs that will allow you to do so and take advantage of them.

These developments will enable you to seem physically younger than your actual age because the body follows the mind. If you think you're younger and act like you're younger, then your body will support that because you'll be doing things to make it true.

In my seventies, I'm doing enormously more through exercise, nutrition, supplements, and other things than I did 30 years ago, and I'm far more conscious and intentional about these things than I was before.

Your "extra years" payoff.
Being conscious of having a greater lifespan means that you're not buying into the status quo of retiring just because you reach a certain age.

Once you've done The Lifetime Extender exercise and come up with your new, higher age number, things you would have thought you didn't have enough time to do will suddenly become achievable because you'll realize you have extra years now in which to do them.

I've seen proof of this with Strategic Coach clients who were planning to wrap up their careers by the time they reached what's considered the usual retirement age, but have instead gone on to work into their eighties.

Amazing things happen when you change your mindset and start to think about the rest of your life not as coming to an end but as constantly getting bigger.

Mindsets attract "miracles."

Being plugged into emerging life extension "miracles" is the direct result of having a mindset that encourages living to an age way beyond the normal average.

Thirty years ago, I wasn't doing the kind of work I can do today. One reason for this is that the technology wasn't there to enable me to do it. As I've embedded myself in the thought of a greater lifetime, I've picked up on not only the technologies related to lifetime extension, but also the technologies that interest me because they allow me to multiply my impact.

Science fiction writer Arthur C. Clarke had this great line: "Any sufficiently advanced technology is indistinguishable from magic." There are technologies and life-extension advancements available today that seemed like science fiction decades ago.

When you get extra years, and they're quality years in which you get to explore, investigate, and experience, it lifts your spirits. All of a sudden, you think longer into the future, and things you thought were impossible become possible.

These changes in mindset become changes in behavior, and that has an impact on others as more people are motivated to adopt that behavior.

Eventually, the behavior reaches critical mass, and people develop the appropriate technology because they know there will be buyers for it. And so the mindset inspires the creation of technology.

Rejuvenating crucial builders.

Once you're tuned in to the latest technologies that will allow you to achieve your goal of an extended lifespan, you'll use them to continually rejuvenate ("make young again").

Your physical health and fitness are made up of a variety of crucial elements that you can think of as building blocks, and you'll always be identifying these building blocks and rejuvenating them with the result that medical tests may show you're physically getting younger as your calendar age gets older.

For the first time, you can disconnect your physical, emotional, and psychological age from your calendar age. Traditionally, these have been intertwined, but they don't need to be. You can't control your calendar age, but you can have some control over your health and the way you feel. You just need to train your brain to find rejuvenating technology.

Technology requires ambition.

Technology is always on the trailing edge of human thought because while it takes time to develop technology, a shift in mindset can happen in seconds.

A lot of people approach things with the attitude, "I'll get interested in this when the capability's there," but it doesn't work that way. If you don't have the interest and the ambition, you'll miss out on everything that's happening.

But if you have a Lifetime Extender mindset, others may follow your example, and the acceleration of the innovation and development of rejuvenating technologies that your ambition brings will extend not only your lifetime but also theirs.

Making longevity longer.

Your personal ambition to live longer, and all of the innovative strategies you undertake to achieve your lifetime extension, contribute to making this a reality for many similarly motivated individuals in the future. It all starts with your having a thought and then a personal goal.

I was alone with my lifetime extension thought for the first six years I was developing it, and by now, I'd estimate that the Lifetime Extender ambition has had an influence on possibly half a billion people.

Adopting the mindset seems to be something that everyone who hears about it wants to do. And the more people that have this ambition, the faster the creation and development of age-reversing technology take place. For examples of some of the technologies and medical breakthroughs I personally take advantage of, visit *strategiccoach.com/go/156*.

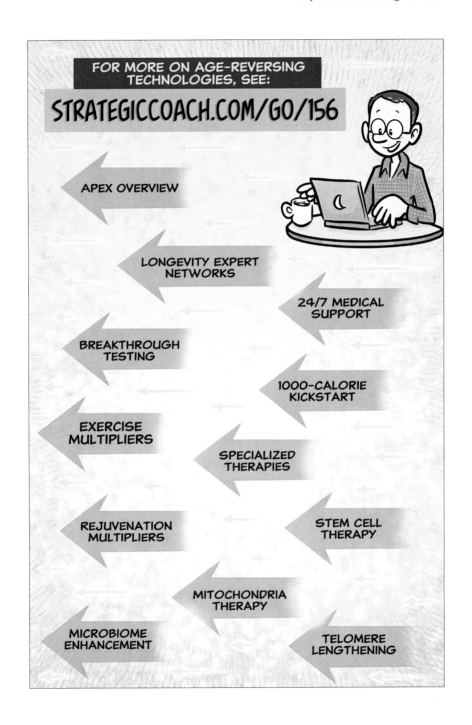

Conclusion
156 Is About Today

You increasingly discover that imaginatively extending your lifetime frees you from being trapped in either the past or the future.

I've noticed that as people reach a certain age, especially around the time they enter their sixties, they start being simultaneously nostalgic about their past and anxious about their future.

They're nostalgic because they have the idea that there was a time when everything was almost perfect, even though they probably didn't feel that way then. Nostalgia is a fiction you tell yourself about a previous time. The past is a thought, not a reality. Nobody has ever lived even a single minute in the past or the future.

Nostalgia is a function of the idea that the time you're currently living in isn't as good as a time you were once living in, and anxiety about the future is the idea that the time you're living in is meaningless because you're running out of time. Anxiety about the future also comes from the feeling that you're running out of crucial factors, including friends, money, and purpose.

But with The Lifetime Extender, you imagine so powerfully that you're going to live longer that it positively impacts you today—and you can truly live in the present.

Sudden immense amount of time.

As you imaginatively create extra years with an extended lifetime number, you'll suddenly feel that an immense amount of time has been added to your future. I've never seen a case where someone did The Lifetime Extender exercise and didn't immediately experience a significant relaxing about time once they had a new sense of an expanding future.

What's more, everyone who does The Lifetime Extender begins to realize that the time they're in is the best time of their life. There's no reason to wait to do all the things you want to do and thought you didn't have time for—the best time to do them is now.

Past becomes strategically useful.
Since you live in the present, which is the only reality, you can engage with the past as it suits you. You can look back at every past experience and find a strategic lesson in it that's useful for your bigger future, which is something you're always creating.

You can do this while being fully aware that the past is just an idea. You can determine how you want to look at a particular part of the past, which may be different from how you experienced it at the time. What you're doing is turning past experiences into useful tools.

That's how I think about it: The only thing about my past that's useful is that it created a lesson I can use in the future. You can only learn and plan in the present, and you can only get smarter if you use the present to learn from the past and to create a bigger future.

Future expands outward from now.
You are now permanently at the center of your entire life, and your future will naturally and continuously expand outward from where you are.

Since I've been in the lifetime extension game, time hasn't been linear for me but rather 360 degrees all around me. This is because I'm not just moving forward, I'm also having an influence on others, which goes out in all directions from where I am.

And this all started with the shift in how I look at the time I have.

Nostalgia and anxiety disappear.

The only time in which you can really live is the present, the "today," and with this lifetime extension mindset, you're going to be increasingly happy in every single "today." All feelings of nostalgia related to the past and all feelings of anxiety related to the future are simply going to disappear.

As a rule, I no longer attend school reunions because everything I needed to learn from my school experience, I've already learned. There's no need for me to go back. When I've gone to a school reunion in the past, I noticed that people there were trying to get meaning out of something that happened sometimes as many as four or five decades ago.

But I've already gotten the meaning and the lessons that can benefit me now, so I'm not nostalgic for the past. And I'm not anxious about the future because my future includes having more friends, having more money, and having more purpose. I stockpile these crucial resources.

"Today" keeps slowing down.

Having gone through The Lifetime Extender exercise, you can see that you're not running out of time, and you know that there's no need to think nostalgically about the past.

You make your past useful, and you're always living in a way that makes for a bigger future.

Time won't speed up for you as the years go by, as it does for so many people. Instead, just the opposite will happen: each "today" in your extended lifetime will slow down in an enjoyable way.

People tell me that as they get older, the years just fly by. If you pay attention to older people, especially those in their sixties or older, you'll see how this attitude results in them not fully living in the present.

All of their behaviors point to the fact that they're either trying to live in the future or else trying to live in some previous time. And both of those times are completely made up ideas that are preventing them from living in the only time they actually have available.

The time flies by for them because there's no day that's actually significant. But this hasn't been my experience at all. The year between my seventy-third and seventy-fourth birthday was the slowest year in my lifetime. It just went on and on—and it was great.

The mindset shift that has come with my goal of living to 156 has changed my life, and I hope The Lifetime Extender changes yours as well.

The only reality is what's happening right now. Recognize that your nostalgia for the past and anxiety about the future are self-created, and live fully in the present.

The Strategic Coach Program
Expanding Entrepreneurial Freedom

The Strategic Coach Program, launched in 1989, has qualifications, measurements, structures, and processes that attract a particular type of talented, successful, and ambitious entrepreneur.

One differentiating quality of these Strategic Coach participants is that they recognize that the technology-empowered 21st century is a unique time to be an entrepreneur. It's the first time that a growing number of individuals with no special birth privileges and no special education can achieve almost anything they set their minds to.

These self-motivated individuals who participate in the three levels of Strategic Coach accept that if they can focus on mastering the right mindsets, they can experience increasing breakthroughs for themselves, both personally and professionally, that are new in history.

The Lifetime Extender is one of these breakthrough mindsets, and there are dozens more for you to master.

Mindsets that enable entrepreneurs to escape.

Many entrepreneurs have the potential and the willingness to achieve exponential goals in the 21st century, but they are blocked from taking action and making progress because they feel trapped in three ways:

• **Trapped thinking:** They are isolated by their own disconnected creativity, which continually churns out ideas that don't translate into achievement. *At Strategic Coach, entrepreneurs increasingly liberate their thinking to create entirely new practical breakthroughs for themselves and others.*

• **Trapped circumstances:** They are surrounded by people who don't support their ambitions, who actively oppose them, or who try to make them feel guilty about their achievements and dreams. *At Strategic Coach, entrepreneurs learn how to increasingly surround themselves with like-minded and like-motivated individuals in every area of their personal and business lives.*

• **Trapped energy:** They're using much of their daily energy to simply sustain themselves without ever actually experiencing exponential performance and results. They wanted to create a growing business but it turns out that they've only created a job—one that always stays the same. *At Strategic Coach, entrepreneurs continually transform every part of their business organizations so that they become self-managing, and then self-multiplying.*

Mindsets that enable entrepreneurs to achieve.

Around the world, the vast majority of entrepreneurs never get out of these trapped circumstances, but at Strategic Coach, our participants not only escape from these limitations, they also jump to extraordinary levels of achievement, success, and satisfaction.

They never stop growing. Strategic Coach participants continually transform how they think, how they make decisions, how they communicate, and how they take action based on their mastery of dozens of unique entrepreneurial mindsets that have been developed in the Program. These are purely entrepreneurial mindsets, like The Lifetime Extender.

We've taken a look at what goes on in the minds of the best

entrepreneurs and have created a thinking system that is custom-designed for them and adjusts to the ambition of each individual.

The Strategic Coach Program provides an accelerating lifetime structure, process, and community for these entrepreneurs to create exponential breakthroughs.

Mindsets that enable entrepreneurs to multiply.

Depending on where you are right now in your life and business, we have a complete set of entrepreneurial mindsets that will immediately jump you up to the next level in terms of your ambition, achievements, and progress. Over the course of your entrepreneurial lifetime, you can move upward through our three levels of mindset measurement and scoring:

1. The Strategic Coach Signature Program: From isolation to teamwork. At this first breakthrough level, you create a "Unique Ability Team" in which everyone does only what they love and do best, allowing you to have a "Self-Managing Company" where your business runs successfully without your having to be involved in the day-to-day operations. Every successful entrepreneur dreams about having this kind of teamwork and organization. Through the Signature level of the Program, these dreams become a reality.

2. The 10x Ambition Program: From teamwork to exponential. You make breakthroughs that transform your life, and your organization becomes a "Self-Multiplying Company." Talented entrepreneurs want to free their biggest growth plans from non-supportive relationships, situations, and circumstances. Through the 10x Ambition level of Strategic Coach, their biggest aspirations attract multiplier capabilities, resources, and opportunities.

3. The Game Changer Program: From exponential to transformative. As your entrepreneurial life becomes exponential, your Self-Multiplying Company become transformative. *The key evidence of this is that your biggest competitors want to become your best students, customers, and promoters.* Game Changer entrepreneurs in Strategic Coach become the leading innovators and cutting-edge teachers in their industries and continually introduce new strategies, methods, and systems that create *new* industries.

Measure yourself, score yourself, get started.

The back cover of this book folds out into a Lifetime Extender Scorecard you can use to score yourself according to the eight mindsets discussed in this book. You can also access a digital copy at *strategiccoach.com/go/156*. Read through the four statements for each mindset and give yourself a score of 1 to 12 based on where your own mindset falls on the spectrum. Put each mindset's score in the first column at the right, and then add up all eight and put the total at the bottom. Now, think about what scores would represent progress over the next quarter. Write these in the second scoring column, add them up, and write in the total.

When you compare the two scores, you can see where you want to go in terms of your achievements and ambitions. If this fast exercise tells you that you want to multiply in all these areas, contact us today to get started:

The Strategic Coach Program is ready for you! Visit us online at *strategiccoach.com* or call us at 416.531.7399 or 1.800.387.3206.

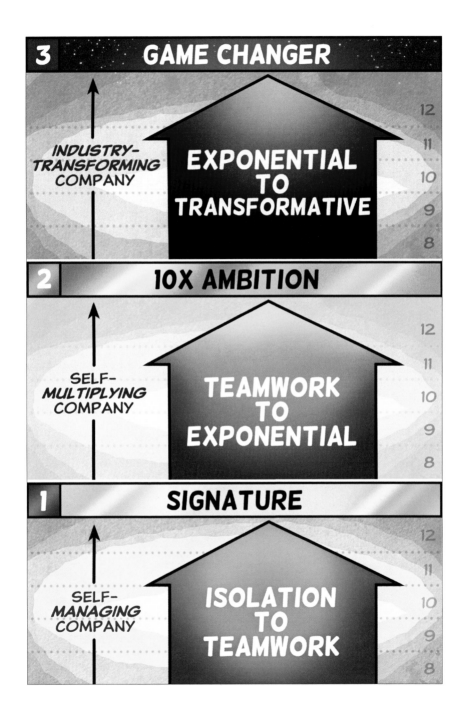

The Lifetime Extender Scorecard

Fold out this Mindset Scorecard and read through the four statements for each mindset. Give yourself a score of 1 to 12 based on where your own mindset falls on the spectrum. Put each mindset's score in the first column at the right, and then add up all eight and put the total at the bottom.

Then, think about what scores would represent progress for you over the next quarter. Write these in the second scoring column, add them up, and write in the total.

When you compare the two scores, you can see where you want to go in terms of your achievements and ambitions.

Mindsets	1	2	3	4	5	6
1 The Lifetime Extender	You never gave any thought to how long you would live, and now you're afraid you don't have much time left.			You increasingly want to get healthier and more fit but you don't know how to think about the best ways to do this.		
2 Everybody Has A Number	You absolutely believe that no one knows when they'll die and you never like thinking about anything related to death.			You would love to extend your life but don't know how to transform this desire into a measurable game plan.		
3 Ignoring Others' Expectations	You've lived your whole life feeling controlled by other people's judgments about how you should think and act.			You know you're living in a period of lifetime extension, but nobody around you would support your interest in this.		
4 Friends, Money, And Purpose	You have always been short on friends, have never had enough money, and are lacking any purpose to get better.			You know that to live longer, you have to improve how you're living right now, but you don't know what factors to focus on.		
5 Eliminating The Idea Of Retirement	You're just hoping that you can free yourself at the end from a lifetime of boring and fatiguing work with irritating people.			You want to keep growing as you get older, but everyone you know has the goal of slowing down and stopping.		
6 Ever-Expanding Happiness	You've always expected other people and things to make your life happier, and you resent that everything has failed.			You know when you're happy and when you're not, but you've never had a way to make greater happiness predictable.		
7 Future Bigger Than Past	You can't remember the last time you felt that your future could be more exciting and energizing.			You've always dreamed about getting bigger and better, but your lack of achievement keeps getting more painful.		
8 Age-Reversing Technology	You find yourself increasingly overwhelmed and oppressed by the scientific and technological promises of longevity.			You're waking up to the possibility of living longer and healthier, but you're afraid that it's already too late for you.		
Scorecard	➡	➡	➡	➡	➡	➡	➡	➡

7	8	9	10	11	12	Score Now	Score Next
You've always lived your life to match those in your age group because you don't expect to live much longer than they do.			You understand that the age at which you expect to die is negotiable — and changing your future number changes your present.				
You live and work with people who rely on their doctors to guide them through to the end of life — and you do too.			You confidently choose the extended age at which you'll die and then use that number to transform everything else.				
You're completely surrounded by people who fully expect to retire, decline, and die in the same way as everyone else.			You pay no attention to how long other people expect to live or what they think about your goal for a longer life.				
You've always planned and created your life to be secure, supported, and satisfied over a normal lifespan.			You continually expand three crucial daily capabilities for living a longer life.				
You're already spending more time thinking about life outside of work than focusing on getting better at your work.			You see yourself becoming increasingly more capable, useful, and productive as your longer life expands.				
You've always contented yourself with improving your material security, comfort, and convenience. That's enough.			You continually identify new areas of happiness in all areas of your life and work, and keep expanding them.				
You accepted long ago that most of your dreams won't happen. You've made your future expectations smaller.			You always see and make your life ahead transformatively bigger and better than all of your previous experience.				
You've trained yourself not to pay attention to any news that makes you uncomfortable about the life you're living.			Your growing motivation for living a longer, more productive life keeps enabling you to feel and act increasingly younger.				

About The Author
Dan Sullivan

Dan Sullivan is the founder and president of The Strategic Coach Inc. and creator of The Strategic Coach® Program, which helps accomplished entrepreneurs reach new heights of success and happiness. He has over 40 years of experience as a strategic planner and coach to entrepreneurial individuals and groups. He is author of over 30 publications, including *The 80% Approach*™, *The Dan Sullivan Question*, *Ambition Scorecard*, *Wanting What You Want*, *The 4 C's Formula*, *The 25-Year Framework*, *The Game Changer*, *The 10x Mind Expander*, *The Mindset Scorecard, The Self-Managing Company*, *Procrastination Priority*, *The Gap And The Gain*, *The ABC Breakthrough*, *Extraordinary Impact Filter*, and *Capableism*, and is co-author with Catherine Nomura of *The Laws of Lifetime Growth*.

Made in United States
North Haven, CT
27 December 2021

13751409R00046